Healing Is My Plan

Healing Is My Plan

DIEDRA WILSON

gatekeeper press
Tampa, Florida

HEALING IS MY PLAN

Published by Gatekeeper Press
7853 Gunn Hwy., Suite 209
Tampa, FL 33626
www.GatekeeperPress.com

Library of Congress Control Number: 2023941301

ISBN (hardcover): 9781662942181
ISBN (paperback): 9781662942198
eISBN: 9781662942204

Welcome!

Meet Diedra Wilson

Diedra R. Wilson is a retired United States Air Force service member and resides in Texas. She filled the role of superintendent in the logistics field and has committed the last 20 years to serving people, leading, and exploring the world.

Diedra has expanded those commitments to sit on panels, be interviewed on podcasts, and teach classes. She has completed her master's degree in Business Administration, several program certifications, and is actively pursuing her doctoral degree in Education.

Diedra is focused on more. She also is an up and coming entrepreneur with her brand Luxe Embrace and her pursuit to become a best-selling author. She has big aspirations and is on the journey to fulfill purpose by following what God has put before her. Diedra's story may not be your story, but we all have one to share!

This activity journal will hopefully help with the healing process before individuals feel exhausted or begin to just give up. I encourage you all to do the work for yourself. Walk with God, identify your pain, and pour into your healing.

"The race is not to the swift, Nor the battle to the strong, Nor bread to the wise, Nor riches to men of understanding, Nor favor to men of skill; But time and chance happen to them all." Ecclesiastes 9:11

 @diedrarenee   /Diedra.renee.5

Table of Contents

Section 1: **Healing + Willing**

    Activity 1: Rebuilding
    Activity 2: Restore
    Activity 3: Trust
    Activity 4: Commitment

Section 2: **Healing + Self**

    Activity 1: Identity
    Activity 2: Renew
    Activity 3: Reflect
    Activity 4: Redeem

Section 3: **Healing + Health**

    Activity 1: Discover
    Activity 2: Dedicate
    Activity 3: Establish
    Activity 4: Resilient

Section 4: **Healing + Wealth**

    Activity 1: Seek
    Activity 2: Change
    Activity 3: Purpose
    Activity 4: Prosper

Healing + Willing

SECTION ONE

This section is an introduction to your will and desire to be open and begin your healing process. There is no time limit; it is all self-paced and self-invested. It will include the following:

- **Repeat Statement** - this is a projection of what you will begin to see within yourself as you do the needed work.

- **Affirmation Statement** - this is a statement of positivity and reassurance of your growth often forgotten.

- **Healing Exercise** - these are activities you can implement within your journey to keep you calm and collected.

Activity 1
REBUILDING

Healing + Willing

"There is a time for everything, and a season for every activity under the heavens: a time to be born and a time to die, a time to plant and a time to uproot, a time to kill and a time to heal, a time to tear down and a time to build, a time to weep and a time to laugh, a time to mourn and a time to dance, a time to scatter stones and a time to gather them, a time to embrace and a time to refrain from embracing, a time to search and a time to give up, a time to keep and a time to throw away, a time to tear and a time to mend, a time to be silent and a time to speak, a time to love and a time to hate, a time for war and a time for peace."
Ecclesiastes 3:1–8

"I'm learning to take time to reflect on the truth in me and the space around me."

Affirm: I am willing to be the best version of me and I am rebuilding who I am.

Healing Exercise: Deep Breathing
(Example: Inhale slowly for 5 secs/exhale slowly for 5 secs. Repeat for 1 min)

Self-Encouragement and Thoughts:

....

....

....

....

....

....

....

....

....

....

....

....

Activity 2
RESTORE

Healing + Willing

"He heals the brokenhearted and binds up their wounds."
Psalms 147:3

"Heal me, LORD, and I will be healed; save me and I will be saved, for you are the one I praise."
Jeremiah 17:14

"I choose forgiveness and I choose healing by letting it go."

Affirm: I am eager to know myself and I am ready to restore the amazing things I have lost within me.

Healing Exercise: Prayer
(Example: Seeking, supplication, and intercession)

Self-Encouragement and Thoughts:

....
....
....
....
....
....
....
....
....
....
....

Activity 3
TRUST

Healing + Willing

*"The righteous cry out, and the LORD hears them;
he delivers them from all their troubles. The LORD is close to the
brokenhearted and saves those who are crushed in spirit.
The righteous person may have many troubles,
but the LORD delivers him from them all; he protects all
his bones, not one of them will be broken. Evil will slay the wicked;
the foes of the righteous will be condemned. The LORD will rescue his
servants; no one who takes refuge in him will be condemned."*
Psalms 34: 17–22

*"And the people all tried to touch him, because power
was coming from him and healing them all."*
Luke 6:19

"I have to trust the power in him and what he has given me."

Affirm: I am enthusiastic as I learn my way and I am becoming whole as I grow.

Healing Exercise: Meditation
(Example: Focusing, mindfulness, and relaxed state)

Self-Encouragement and Thoughts:

....
....
....
....
....
....
....
....
....
....
....

Healing Is My Plan || Journal

Activity 4
COMMITMENT

Healing + Willing

*"If my people, who are called by my name,
will humble themselves and pray and seek my face and turn
from their wicked ways, then I will hear from heaven, and I will forgive
their sin and will heal their land."*
2 Chronicles 7:14

"I will slowly open my pain and let healing come in."

Affirm: I am committed to my journey
and I am refining my character.

Healing Exercise: Conserve your energy
(Example: Search for peace within)

Self-Encouragement and Thoughts:

....
....
....
....
....
....
....
....
....
....
....
....

What's on Your Mind?

....
....
....
....
....
....
....
....
....
....
....
....
....
....
....
....
....
....
....
....
....
....
....

Healing + Self

SECTION TWO

This section is an introduction of you (self) wanting to identify the trauma, disappointment, and hurt during your life journey. It will include the following:

- **Repeat Statement**- this is a projection of what you will begin to see within yourself as you do the needed work.

- **Affirmation Statement**- this is a statement of positivity and reassurance of your growth often forgotten.

- **Healing Exercise**- these are activities you can implement within your journey to keep you calm and collected.

Activity 1
IDENTITY

Healing + Self

"The LORD is my shepherd, I lack nothing. He makes me lie down in green pastures, he leads me beside quiet waters, he refreshes my soul. He guides me along the right paths for his name's sake. Even though I walk through the darkest valley, I will fear no evil, for you are with me; your rod and your staff, they comfort me. You prepare a table before me in the presence of my enemies. You anoint my head with oil; my cup overflows. Surely your goodness and love will follow me all the days of my life, and I will dwell in the house of the LORD forever."
Psalms 23

"I know who I am and whom I belong to."

Affirm: I am repairing my mind and my heart while identifying what I truly need.

Healing Exercise: Relax
(Example: Rest)

Self-Encouragement and Thoughts:

....
....
....
....
....
....
....
....
....
....
....
....

Activity 2
RENEW

Healing + Self

*"So do not fear, for I am with you; do not be dismayed,
for I am your God. I will strengthen you and help you;
I will uphold you with my righteous right hand."*
Isaiah 41:10

"My journey is specifically for me and I will keep going."

Affirm: I am renewing my soul
and I am building my individuality.

Healing Exercise: Play soothing and motivating music
(Example: Lo-fi, gospel, jazz or instrumental)

Self-Encouragement and Thoughts:

....
....
....
....
....
....
....
....
....
....
....

Activity 3
REFLECT

Healing + Self

"Lord, by such things people live; and my spirit finds life in them too.
You restored me to health and let me live."
Isaiah 38:16

"But those who hope in the LORD will renew their strength.
They will soar on wings like eagles; they will run and not grow weary,
they will walk and not be faint."
Isaiah 40:31

"I will praise thee; for I am fearfully and wonderfully made:
marvellous are thy works; and that my soul knoweth right well."
Psalm 139:14

"To live is to learn and to learn is to grow."

Affirm: I am progressing in my inner self, and my outer dispositions are a reflection of my evolution.

Healing Exercise: Read a snippet
(Example: Daily devotional or self-improvement guide)

Self-Encouragement and Thoughts:

....
....
....
....
....
....
....
....
....
....
....
....

Activity 4
REDEEM

Healing + Self

*"Dear friend, I pray that you may enjoy
good health and that all may go well with you,
even as your soul is getting along well."*
3 John 1:2

"My mind, body, and soul are as one. So am I."

Affirm: I am redeeming the beautiful spirit in me, and I am discovering the fine details that define who I am.

Healing Exercise: Enjoy something fun
(Example: Comedy show, family time or play games)

Self-Encouragement and Thoughts:

....
....
....
....
....
....
....
....
....
....
....
....

The Way I Love Me!
(insert below)

What's on Your Mind?

Healing + Health

SECTION THREE

This section is an introduction reminding you to pour into your well-being and to be mindful of healthy changes in your regime.

It will include the following:

- **Repeat Statement**- this is a projection of what you will begin to see within yourself as you do the needed work.

- **Affirmation Statement**- this is a statement of positivity and reassurance of your growth often forgotten.

- **Healing Exercise**- these are activities you can implement within your journey to keep you calm and collected.

Activity 1
DISCOVER

Healing + Health

*"He gives strength to the weary and increases
the power of the weak."*
Isaiah 40:29

*"'But I will restore you to health and heal your wounds,'
declares the LORD."*
Jeremiah 30:17

"My struggles do not define me, but my strength to heal does."

Affirm: I am restoring my will to conquer my fears and use my power within to keep me steady.

Healing Exercise: Conserve your energy
(Example: Search for peace within)

Self-Encouragement and Thoughts:

....

....

....

....

....

....

....

....

....

....

....

....

Activity 2
DEDICATE

Healing + Health

"My flesh and my heart may fail, but God is the strength of my heart and my portion forever."
Psalms 73:26

"Praise the LORD, my soul, and forget not all his benefits — who forgives all your sins and heals all your diseases, who redeems your life from the pit and crowns you with love and compassion."
Psalms 103:2–4

"Be kind to myself and be loving toward myself."

Affirm: I am dedicated to the fullness of my being, and I am passionate on speaking life into myself.

Healing Exercise: Deep breathing

(Example: Inhale slowly for 5 secs/exhale slowly for 5 secs. Repeat for 1 min)

Self-Encouragement and Thoughts:

....
....
....
....
....
....
....
....
....
....
....

Activity 3
ESTABLISH

Healing + Health

"LORD my God, I called to you for help, and you healed me."
Psalms 30:2

"Then they cried to the LORD in their trouble, and he saved them from their distress. He sent out his word and healed them; he rescued them from the grave. Let them give thanks to the LORD for his unfailing love and his wonderful deeds for mankind."
Psalms 107:19–21

"I am fearfully and wonderfully made in my creator's eyes."

Affirm: I am whole in my insecurities,
and I am a living testimony of resiliency.

Healing Exercise: Meditation
(Example: Focusing, mindfulness, and relaxed state)

Self-Encouragement and Thoughts:

....
....
....
....
....
....
....
....
....
....
....
....

Activity 4
RESILIENT

Healing + Health

*"Come to me, all you who are weary and burdened,
and I will give you rest. Take my yoke upon you and learn from me,
for I am gentle and humble in heart,
and you will find rest for your souls.
For my yoke is easy and my burden is light."*
Matthew 11:28–30

"I have permission to live and forgive myself of my shortcomings."

Affirm: I am reestablishing my thought process, and I am comfortable with being a resource to myself.

Healing Exercise: Prayer
(Example: Seeking, supplication, and intercession)

Self-Encouragement and Thoughts:

....
....
....
....
....
....
....
....
....
....
....

Be Kind to You
Weekday Calendar

Write down the nice things you did for yourself the day you did it.
A reminder to be good to you during your process

Monday:

Tuesday:

Wednesday:

Thursday:

Friday:

Saturday:

Sunday

What's on Your Mind?

....
....
....
....
....
....
....
....
....
....
....
....
....
....
....
....
....
....
....
....
....
....

Healing + Wealth

SECTION FOUR

This section is an introduction to contentment and balance with your spiritual health and defining what it means to you in this process. It will include the following:

- **Repeat Statement**- this is a projection of what you will begin to see within yourself as you do the needed work.

- **Affirmation Statement**- this is a statement of positivity and reassurance of your growth often forgotten.

- **Healing Exercise**- these are activities you can implement within your journey to keep you calm and collected.

Activity 1
SEEK

Healing + Wealth

"LORD, be gracious to us; we long for you. Be our strength
every morning, our salvation in time of distress."
Isaiah 33:2

"But seek first his kingdom and his righteousness,
and all these things will be given to you as well."
Matthew 6:33

"Peace I leave with you; my peace I give you.
I do not give to you as the world gives. Do not let your hearts
be troubled and do not be afraid."
John 14:27

"In my still moment, I will find my inner peace and joy."

Affirm: I am establishing a new behavior and seeking the treasures that have always been in my heart and mind.

Healing Exercise: Play soothing and motivating music
(Example: Lo-fi, gospel, jazz or instrumental)

Self-Encouragement and Thoughts:

....

....

....

....

....

....

....

....

....

....

....

Activity 2
CHANGE

Healing + Wealth

"Then your light will break forth like the dawn, and your healing will quickly appear; then your righteousness will go before you, and the glory of the LORD will be your rear guard."
Isaiah 58:8

"Let perseverance finish its work so that you may be mature and complete, not lacking anything."
James 1:4

*"Let the light in me shine bright so all can see.
And I will believe others can receive the same fulfillment."*

Affirm: I am ready to continue in my change
and move in my favor as my wounds heal.

Healing Exercise: Enjoy something fun
(Example: Comedy show, family time or play games)

Self-Encouragement and Thoughts:

....
....
....
....
....
....
....
....
....
....
....
....

Activity 3
PURPOSE

Healing + Wealth

"Hear, LORD, and be merciful to me; LORD, be my help."
You turned my wailing into dancing; you removed my sackcloth
and clothed me with joy."
Psalms 30: 10–11

"Gracious words are a honeycomb, sweet to the soul
and healing to the bones."
Proverbs 16:24

"Diligence is key to a successful change.
It may not be easy but it's worth it."

Affirm: I am releasing all that halts my progress and will remain in my purpose.

Healing Exercise: Read a snippet
(Example: Daily devotional or self-improvement guide)

Self-Encouragement and Thoughts:

....

....

....

....

....

....

....

....

....

....

....

....

Activity 4
PROSPER

Healing + Wealth

"Nevertheless, I will bring health and healing to it; I will heal my people and will let them enjoy abundant peace and security."
Jeremiah 33:6

"And my God will meet all your needs according to the riches of his glory in Christ Jesus."
Philippians 4:19

"My riches are within and that itself is enough."

Affirm: I am refining my views and thoughts of myself, while having prosperity.

Healing Exercise: Relax
(Example: Rest)

Self-Encouragement and Thoughts:

....
....
....
....
....
....
....
....
....
....
....
....

Be Kind to Others
Weekday Calendar

Write down the nice things you did for someone else.
A reminder to be kind to other peoples' process

Monday:

Tuesday:

Wednesday:

Thursday:

Friday:

Saturday:

Sunday

What's on Your Mind?

....
....
....
....
....
....
....
....
....
....
....
....
....
....
....
....
....
....
....
....
....
....
....
....

Healing Is My Plan || Journal

Printed in the USA
CPSIA information can be obtained
at www.ICGtesting.com
LVHW072352021123
762705LV00013B/7